Onward

A Photobiography of African-American
Polar Explorer Matthew Henson

by Dolores Johnson

NATIONAL GEOGRAPHIC
WASHINGTON, D.C.

To my cousin, Robbie McClure—D.J.

Published by the National Geographic Society
John M. Fahey, Jr., *President and Chief Executive Officer*
Gilbert M. Grosvenor, *Chairman of the Board*
Nina D. Hoffman, *Executive Vice President, President of Books and Education Publishing Group*
Ericka Markman, *Senior Vice President, President of Children's Books and Education Publishing Group*

Staff for This Book
Nancy Laties Feresten, *Vice President, Editor-in-Chief of Children's Books*
Jennifer Emmett, *Project Editor*
Bea Jackson, *Art Director, Children's Books*
David M. Seager, *Art Director*
Marty Ittner, *Designer*
Daniel L. Sherman, *Illustrations Editor*
Janet Dustin, *Illustrations Coordinator*
Carl Mehler, *Director of Maps*
Joseph F. Ochlak, *Map Researcher*
Gregory Ugiansky and Tibor G. Tóth, *Map Production*
Margo Browning, *Copy Editor*
Connie D. Binder, *Indexer*
R. Gary Colbert, *Production Director*
Lewis R. Bassford, *Production Manager*
Vincent P. Ryan, Alan V. Kerr, *Manufacturing Managers*

Copyright © 2006 National Geographic Society

All rights reserved. Reproduction of the whole or any part of the contents without written permission from the National Geographic Society is strictly prohibited.

Library of Congress Cataloging-in-Publication Data
Johnson, Dolores, 1949-
Onward : a photobiography of African-American polar explorer Matthew Henson / by Dolores Johnson.
   p. cm.
Includes bibliographical references.
ISBN 0-7922-7914-X (trade) — ISBN 0-7922-7915-8 (library)
1. Henson, Matthew Alexander, 1866-1955—Juvenile literature.
2. African American explorers—Biography—Juvenile literature.
3. North Pole—Discovery and exploration—Juvenile literature.
I. Title.
G635.H4J63 2005
0910'.92—dc22
                     2005005837

Acknowledgments
The publisher gratefully acknowledges the assistance of Francille Rusan Wilson, Ph.D., of the African American Studies department at the University of Maryland, for reviewing and commenting on the text and layout.

FRONT COVER: A remarkable determination and strength of character are displayed in the face of Matthew Henson.

HALF-TITLE PAGE: Matthew Henson, in silhouette, is shown driving a sledge (sled) dog team past towering drifts of snow.

TITLE PAGE: Matthew Henson drives his sledge onward with determination toward the North Pole, overcoming the obstacles of sacrifice, isolation and deprivation in his path.

OPPOSITE PAGE: A man born poor in rural Maryland became enthralled by a life of adventure. He resolved to become part of history—and he did.

All photographs from the Robert E. Peary Collection, National Geographic Society, except as noted:

Trade edition case cover, Paul Nicklen/National Geographic Image Collection; Page: 10 (upper), Maryland Historical Society; 10 (lower), courtesy The Library of Congress; 11, Maryland Historical Society; 12 (lower), CORBIS; 12 (background), CORBIS; 19 (background), *New York Times*; 32, CORBIS; 46, Sisse Brimberg; 50, Joseph H. Bailey, NGS; 52 (background), Joseph H. Bailey; 53, Bettmann/CORBIS; 54, Hulton-Dutch Collection/CORBIS; 55 (upper, inset), Bettmann/CORBIS; 55 (lower, inset), Bettmann/CORBIS; 55 (background), *New York Times*; 57, Bettmann/CORBIS; 58, Dr. Allen S. Counter; 60 (LO), Bettmann/CORBIS; 61, Bob Sacha/NGS; 62, courtesy Daniel Sherman Collection.

The body text of the book is set in Filosofia.
The display text is set in Ovidius Light and Keedy Sans.

Printed in the United States of America

"The lure of the Arctic is tugging at my heart..."

FROM MATTHEW HENSON'S GRAVESTONE

Leila Savoy Andrade, a former security officer for the National Geographic Society, is shown holding a picture of her great-great-great uncle, Matthew Henson. She stands in front of a flag that was carried on his various North Pole expeditions.

Foreword

Growing up with an explorer in the family—even one who died long before I was born—always made life just a little more exciting. There was the pride of knowing someone in my own family had done something important. There was the inspiration when it came to my own adventures. Best of all, there were the stories—oh, how I loved the stories! I would always ask my grandmother to tell me more about our family's explorer, my great-great-great uncle, Matthew Henson. It didn't matter to me that not everyone I knew had heard of him. I knew that Matthew Henson had stood at the North Pole in 1909, before anyone else. And I always though that was pretty special.

I felt an even greater connection to Matthew Henson when I went to work at the National Geographic Society. I was a security guard in the very halls that sponsored explorers on expeditions to all the far reaches of the world. It took the National Geographic Society a long while to give Matthew Henson the same recognition they gave to Admiral Robert E. Peary, the leader of the North Pole expedition. In 2001 the Society awarded Matthew Henson the Hubbard Medal, their highest honor for exploration. It was the first Hubbard Medal ever awarded posthumously.

At the Matthew Henson Earth Conservation Center on the Anacostia River in Washington, D.C., I witnessed the ceremony along with other family members. I was proud that the stories I knew so well from childhood, the stories of this brave adventurer who persevered against many obstacles to achieve his goal, were beginning to be told.

—LEILA SAVOY ANDRADE

MATTHEW HENSON, BORN ON AUGUST 8, 1866, began life at a momentous time in American history. The Civil War had just ended, and the U.S. government was beginning to institute the policy of Reconstruction. This strategy was intended to reorganize the war-torn South and help the newly freed slaves. African Americans were optimistic that the end of slavery would bring about equality with white people, but the newly won rights of black citizens began to evaporate. Disorder was unleashed in southern state governments. Angry white groups formed to terrorize African Americans into forfeiting their civil rights (the personal liberties guaranteed by the Constitution). Riots inflamed many southern cities. An era of expectation deteriorated into a time of turmoil.

Matthew Henson was born in Charles County, Maryland, a state that had been a slave state, yet had not left the Union. Though never enslaved, Matthew's parents, Lemuel and Carolyn, still had to claw out a desperate existence as sharecroppers. They did not own the land on which they farmed tobacco but rented the land from a large landowner and paid him with a share of the meager proceeds from their crop. When Matthew was not even two years old, Lemuel and Carolyn decided to move their three children 30 miles to Washington, D.C., to escape from the poverty and racial turmoil.

When Matthew was seven years old, his mother died and his father remarried. Six years later, his father was killed in a farming accident, leaving the boy completely on his own. Matthew left school and found a job as a dishwasher. Within months, the strong-willed, independent boy was bored with the menial jobs of busing tables and washing dishes. One day in 1879, Matthew met a grizzled old sailor named Baltimore Jack. The sailor filled the boy's head with rollicking tales of the wonders of the sea and the joys of living a life filled with adventure. Days later, Matthew said goodbye to dishwashing. He was only 13 when he walked the 40 miles to the port city of Baltimore, Maryland.

Matthew Henson is shown in a casual pose on the deck of the ship, the *Roosevelt*, the ship that took Henson and explorer Robert E. Peary on their 1905–06 expedition to the North Pole. Peary once wrote: "Henson was the best man I had with me for this type of work. . . ."

Top: A sharecropper's house was not much more than a one-room shack with a dirt or wood floor. Henson's family share-cropped on a tobacco farm, much like the people in the lower image. The labor was exhausting, tough, and poorly paid.

Matthew was in awe of the bustling port filled with ships loading and unloading cargo, readying to sail to far-off lands. While wandering the harbor, Matthew met a sea captain. He boldly asked the elderly white man for a job. Captain Childs was impressed by Matthew's intelligence and resolve. He hired him as a cabin boy on the spot.

Aboard the steamship, *Katie Hines*, bound for Hong Kong with a load of wheat, Matthew was kept busy every day helping the cook prepare and serve meals and keeping the captain's cabin in order. However, after the day's chores were completed, Captain Childs took Matthew aside for two hours every day to teach him reading, writing, geography, history, carpentry, and how to navigate by the stars.

During his years aboard ship, Matthew visited China, Japan, and Manila, in the Philippines, as well as North Africa, Spain, France, and southern Russia. While he was a sailor, Matthew Henson grew from a small, skinny child into a muscular, confident young man with a distinct appetite for adventure.

Then misfortune struck. In 1883, Captain Childs died, and Henson was forced to look for work on other

While a teenager, Matthew Henson was convinced that a seaman's life was a life of adventure. He walked 40 miles to Baltimore to become a sailor.

sailing ships. Two years later, sick of fellow sailors calling him racial names and taunting him with insults, Henson left sailing. He found work over the next two years as a watchman, dockworker, chauffeur, messenger boy, and bellhop.

It wasn't until 1887, while Henson was working as a stock boy at the B. J. Steinmetz & Sons hat store in Washington, D.C., that his life turned around. One day the store manager called him to the front counter to introduce him to a young naval lieutenant named Robert Edwin Peary. The lieutenant had been ordered to take a survey expedition to Central America and was looking for a manservant who would keep his clothes and quarters clean. Henson's employer had recommended him. Henson eagerly agreed to take the job.

Henson had visited the tropics in his seafaring days, so he was probably not surprised by Nicaragua's hot, humid jungle. Peary and Henson arrived, accompanied by hundreds of Jamaican laborers who they shipped in to hack a path through jungle made nearly impenetrable by dense clusters of broad-leafed trees studding mud-filled swamps. Once the path was cleared, surveyors laid out the route for a canal that was proposed to compete with a

Top: Naval officer Robert Peary (upper left) hired Matthew Henson (upper right) as his manservant in 1887. They went to the jungles of Nicaragua to survey a proposed canal between the Atlantic and Pacific Oceans, below. Background: Dense foliage; deep, raging streams; and a heavy insect infestation made the survey a challenge. The map opposite shows the proposed route of the canal that was never built, due to its lengthy route too close to volcanoes.

potential canal through Panama. The canals would allow ships to sail from the Atlantic to the Pacific Oceans without going around South America.

Henson's job in Nicaragua became more than just keeping Lieutenant Peary in clean clothes and comfortable living quarters. Like Captain Childs before him, Peary appreciated Henson's intelligence and grit. When Peary's chainman became ill, he gave Henson the job. Peary used a magnetic compass to help him sort out the best transit route through the jungle. Henson held a surveyor's chain taut in a precise position to ensure the accuracy of Peary's calculations, much like a chain is held during football games today to measure first downs. Though he had to perform his task while standing in waist-deep mud and dodging swarms of mosquitoes, Henson thrived in his job. He no longer felt like a servant.

When the two adventurers returned to the States, Peary went back to the Navy and busied himself making plans for his next adventure. For 400 years, explorers had attempted to be the first to set foot at the geographical top of the world, the North Pole. But no one had made it there and survived to tell the story. Peary wanted to place his name in history as the first to reach the North Pole.

Henson could find no work when he returned home. Nostalgic for the intensity of his Nicaraguan adventure, he wrote to Peary in August 1888 asking if the lieutenant planned to return to South America. But Peary did not reply.

Months later, Henson sent another letter to Peary. He told his former employer that he would be willing to stay in Nicaragua as long as Peary stayed. Because Henson received no response from Peary, he finally went back to his old job at Steinmetz & Sons.

Finally, early in 1889, Lieutenant Peary wrote to Henson asking if he would be interested in working as a messenger at the League Island Navy Yard in Philadelphia where Peary had recently been reassigned. Henson readily agreed and moved to Philadelphia.

Henson had grown comfortable in Washington, D.C., living with his sister, Eliza, and her family. He found it more difficult to fit into Philadelphia's African-American society. There were few organizations or clubs he could join if he did not work in certain jobs, such as janitorial or engineering. So he approached the most hospitable organization in the black community, the church. There, strangers were welcomed and invited to social events. Henson met and started dating Eva Helen Flint, a stylish, 22-year-old sales clerk. Eventually, thoughts of his next big adventure became secondary to planning a wedding and saving enough money to buy a new home for the two of them.

In February of 1891, Peary summoned Henson to his office. The Navy had given the lieutenant a leave of absence so that he could explore northwest Greenland. Peary was particularly interested in Greenland because he thought it would be a good place to launch his attempt to reach the North Pole. Peary asked Henson to come along as his personal assistant. He offered Henson only $50 (just over $900 today) for the entire year's work. The lieutenant warned of the dangers and suggested that Henson's African heritage—as a "son of the Equator"—would make the Arctic climate difficult for him. "I'll go North with you, sir, and I think I'll stand it as well as any man," Henson told him.

Eva tried to dissuade Henson from going to the Arctic, but Henson understood that this was his opportunity to make history, and he was determined to take it. Eva gave in. On April 16, 1891, they were married. For two months the couple lived with her family while they waited for the expedition to depart.

On June 6, 1891, Henson, Peary, and the rest of the members of the expedition boarded a ship out of Brooklyn, New York, named the *Kite*. The other crew members were a diverse lot with various levels of experience. They were Frederick A. Cook, a New York doctor; Eivind Astrup, a Norwegian ski champion; John T. Verhoeff, an athlete (who paid $2,000 to be on the expedition); Langdon Gibson, an ornithologist; and Josephine Peary, Peary's wife, an unusual addition since most people then believed that white women were too delicate to survive in the Arctic.

The *Kite* sailed for about a month before it reached northern Greenland. Towering icebergs studded the route through Baffin Bay. Then, on July 11, a spectacular incident threatened the entire expedition. While ramming through the bay, the rudder of the *Kite* struck a piece of ice, tearing the tiller from the hands of the two men on duty. The tiller slapped across the deck, striking Peary and breaking two bones in his right leg. Henson helped carry Peary to his cabin, where Dr. Cook set his leg in a cast. The lieutenant refused to cancel the expedition. He was so determined that the ship remain on course, he slept with a compass by his bed to make sure that the crew obeyed his orders.

The *Kite* arrived at McCormick Bay's red, lichen-covered cliffs in late July. Crew members brought Peary onto the shore on a plank. Henson began construction of the two-room house, nicknamed "Red Cliff House," in which the expedition would live.

Mountainous icebergs and ice floes studded the waters of Baffin Bay, making navigation extremely treacherous. This photo is the view seen from the deck of either the expedition ship, the *Kite*, or a later ship, the *Falcon*.

15

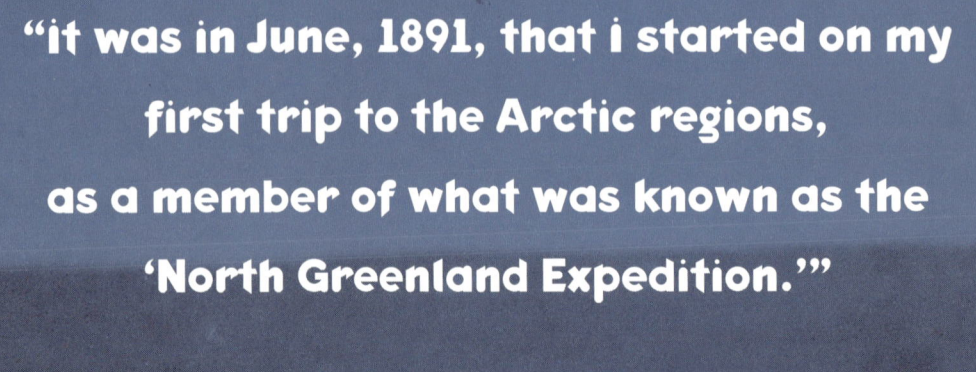

"It was in June, 1891, that I started on my first trip to the Arctic regions, as a member of what was known as the 'North Greenland Expedition.'"

Mrs. Josephine Peary is shown departing by rowboat for the *Kite*, visible in the background. She is looking at Red Cliff House, perhaps saying farewell to her husband, Lieutenant Peary, who is, more than likely, the photographer.

third of the structure was partitioned off for the Pearys. The other two-thirds, heated by a pot-bellied stove, was to be home to the remaining crew. When the house was ready, the *Kite* sailed home, leaving the explorers behind.

The house was named after the red lichen that colored the steep cliffs near the bay. As it was summer, the sun shone for almost 20 hours a day at this high altitude. Upon arrival, the visitors viewed a land that was desolate and bare of trees, though still sprinkled with spring's meager growth of grass and flowers. Fortunately, the *Kite* had carried timber for house and sledge (sled) construction and basic food supplies. The crew members supplemented their rations by setting traps and hunting for fox, walrus, and deer for their meat and fur.

While it was Henson's primary job to build the house, others worked on convincing Inuit families to live close to headquarters. Peary felt that the Inuit (also known as Eskimos or Esquimos) could provide the expedition with materials and knowledge of how to survive in the challenging environment. The first Inuit to approach the visitors were a man named Ikwah and his wife, Mané. When they saw Henson for the first time, they ran to him saying, "Inuit…Inuit" in delight. Seeing his skin color was about the same as their own, they assumed he must be one of them. Henson threw his arms around Ikwah and hugged him.

The Inuit (meaning "the People") live farther north than any other people. At that time, the only property they owned was their dogs, weapons, and tools. The only food they ate was the meat, blood, and blubber from animals they hunted. Though nomads, the Inuit the expedition members encountered lived sheltered lives. They had rarely seen a living tree (since trees don't grow this far north) and considered wood the most valuable resource after food. Money was of no use to them. They bartered their goods or shared what they acquired with one another. The only education boys received was training to hunt and to drive the sledges. Girls were taught how to sew fur garments, keep the lamp burning, and prepare the food and water.

Though the Inuit had lived in the far north for centuries, they had never ventured across the frozen Arctic Ocean toward the North Pole. They believed that if a hunter stepped too far out on the ice pack, the devil, Torngak, would destroy him. It was not until the *Oopernadleet*—"the visitors who come in the spring"—arrived with their gifts of tools, weapons, and blankets that the Inuit considered traveling to the North Pole.

"...the Esquimo travels heavy and takes his women and children with him as a matter of course."

At left is the Inuit woman Mané, the wife of Ikwah, and her two children, Annadore and Nowyahrtlik (in the back pouch) next to Mrs. Josephine Peary. As the women stand next to each other, the contrast in their height, posture, and dress is remarkable.

The Inuit saw a brother in Matthew Henson not only because of his skin color but because he, of all those in the expedition, chose to learn their language and their way of life. They shared their survival skills with him, and he, in turn, taught Peary and the rest of the crew. The Inuit taught Henson to wear and sleep in fur clothing and to slip moss into his sealskin boots as protection from the cold. They taught him how to build and drive their sledges, and he became the best sledge driver on the expedition.

Each sledge was dragged by eight dogs tied together in a fan formation. The sledge driver drove the most dominant dog onward with the skillful snap of a whip. The other dogs followed their leader.

After months of hunting for food and building sledges, it was time to start out. In April 1892, Peary assigned crews to break a trail northward and cache, or store, supplies along the trail. Each trail-breaking crew, composed of Inuit and expedition members, would move supplies ahead, then return to base camp, thus conserving food and fuel so the teams behind them could advance farther north. If all went well, Peary, with a final team, could then follow the trail, breaking only the last part, and reach the North Pole.

On May 24, Peary recruited the young Norwegian, Eivind Astrup, to begin the final advance to the Pole. The two men headed northeast, crossing the interior of Greenland. The rest of the expedition remained at Red Cliff House. Because he was the best sledge driver, Henson had hoped to be part of the final team, but he was ordered to remain at Red Cliff House as well. His duties were to hunt for fresh meat and serve as housekeeper, cook, and general handyman for Mrs. Peary.

The *Kite* returned to pick up the expedition in the first week of August, but the lieutenant and Astrup had not yet returned. Before Henson could assemble a rescue party, the two men staggered into camp emaciated and exhausted. They had not reached the Pole but had managed to sledge north for 500 miles and had arrived at a 3,000-foot-high mountain Peary named Navy Cliff. Peary believed that this was the northernmost shore of Greenland.

As the *Kite* was preparing to depart, Henson realized that John Verhoeff had not returned from a two-day hike searching for rock specimens. He organized a search party. After six days of looking, the search party found footprints beside a deep crack in the ice called a crevasse, and concluded

Top: Henson (right) and the Inuit Annowkah, are dressed in fur skins that cover every inch of their bodies but their faces. They are hauling a sled of deerskins after a hunt. Below: Men pause while driving a sledge pulled by teams of dogs harnessed in a fan formation.

"...the journey to the Pole and back is not to be regarded as a pleasure outing, and our so-called jaunt was by no means a cake-walk."

that Verhoeff had fallen in and died. They abandoned the search and returned to the ship, which brought the expedition back to the States.

Peary went on a series of lecture tours to raise funds for the next expedition. He decorated the stage like an Inuit village and dressed himself in furs and boots. Henson joined Peary in fundraising. To the sound of Peary's "*Huk, huk,*" Henson drove a barking, howling dog team onto the stage with the snap of his whip. The two men raised so much money in 165 appearances that they were back in New York by the spring of 1893, planning the next expedition.

Members of the 1891-92 expedition build a shelter in the snow as two American flags fly from skis.

In the summer of 1893, Peary's Second Greenland Expedition sailed on a ship named the *Falcon*, arriving at Inglefield Gulf on August 3. There they constructed a house nicknamed "Anniversary Lodge." Josephine Peary again accompanied the expedition, but this time she was six months pregnant and brought with her a woman named Mrs. Cross to act as baby nurse. Henson and Eivind Astrup, both veterans of the 1891 expedition, were the only experienced crew members in a group of 11 men and two women, not including Inuit. In bringing a crew this large, Peary was taking a risk. More crew members meant more people to do the work of the expedition, but also more mouths to feed.

On September 12, 1893, Josephine Peary gave birth in Anniversary Lodge to the first white child born that far north. The baby was named Marie Ahnighito Peary. ("Ahnighito" was a female Inuit name.) Inuit traveled for miles to see the blue-eyed, blond "Snow Baby."

Left: Drivers, a sledge, and dogs pass a crevasse, or giant crack in the ice, a common hazard in Arctic travel. Such natural ice formations could be huge and were very dangerous if someone should fall into the deep fissure.

A young child came into Henson's life, as well. He was an orphan boy named Kudlooktoo, whose mother had recently died. Allowing Henson to adopt Kudlooktoo showed the Inuit's affection for Henson, whom they called Maripahluk, or "Matthew, the Kind One." Inuit children were loved and pampered by everyone, and there were Inuit who wanted to adopt Kudlooktoo. But they stepped aside in favor of Henson. Certainly the explorer cared deeply for the boy. He bathed him, cut his hair, began to teach him English, and made him a bed of furs next to his own. But when Henson returned to America, Kudlooktoo stayed behind.

Nothing seemed to go right for the expedition. Astrup and two other crewmen who had advanced to cache supplies were caught halfway up the side of a glacier in a snowstorm. While Peary and Henson were gone to retrieve them, a freak wave from the bay smashed most of the barrels that held the fuel. Hugh Lee, a newspaperman, wandered away in the storm and couldn't be found for three days. The intensity of the storms increased. Finally, in March, a party of seven men headed north to cache supplies. But again, storms raged, and several crew members were driven back to base camp with injuries or illness.

On April 10, after so many near catastrophes, Peary decided to halt the expedition. The crew buried their extra supplies and marked them with nine-foot-tall poles so that the materials would be available for the next trip across the ice pack.

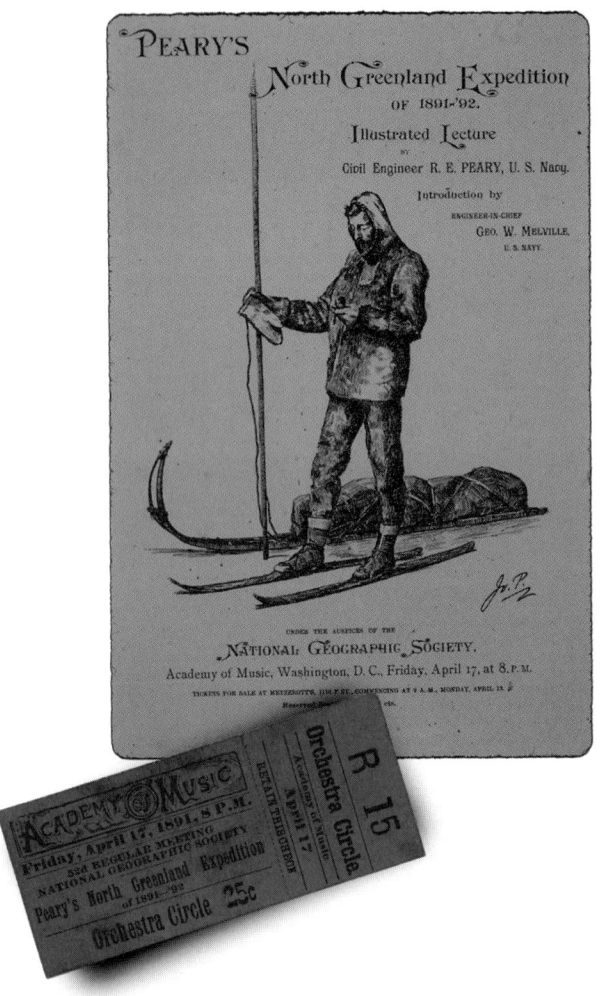

An advertisement and ticket to one of Robert Peary's fund-raising lectures for his 1891-92 Arctic expedition.

Peary decided to remain in Greenland when the *Falcon* came in August 1894 to pick up the 11 crew members and Peary's family. He asked for volunteers to stay with him. Only Henson and Hugh Lee, the newspaperman, decided to stay.

The *Falcon* had brought few supplies on its return since the captain didn't know that Peary intended to remain in the Arctic. But Peary wasn't worried. They had the supplies that they had marked with the nine-foot poles. But after the ship left, the three remaining team members could not retrieve their cached supplies because eight feet of ice and snow covered them. Henson hunted for venison and walrus meat to tide them over.

Henson, Peary, and Lee, briefly accompanied by six Inuit, began their first advance to the North Pole on April 1, 1895. However, storms delayed them, and the food began to run out. The men soon began to slaughter the weakest dogs to feed both men and the other dogs. The assault on the Pole was no longer the priority—returning to the base camp became vital to survival. Once again Hugh Lee became separated from the other two men as Henson broke the trail ahead. When he was finally found, Lee was so sick from hunger and frostbite that he had to be left behind in a tent while Peary and Henson hunted for musk oxen. This hunt very nearly put an end to Peary and the remaining team.

Top: Josephine Peary holds her approximately 3-month-old infant, Marie Ahnighito Peary, nicknamed "Snow Baby," who was born in the Arctic. The baby attracted a number of amazed Inuit who had never seen a blue-eyed, blond baby. Below: A picture of her father, Robert E. Peary, was taken about the time of his final expedition.

"...for periods covering more than twelve months, I have been to all intents an Esquimo, with Esquimos for companions, speaking their language, dressing in the same kind of clothes, living in the same kind of dens, eating the same food, enjoying their pleasures, and frequently sharing their griefs."

Robert Peary would encourage entire Inuit families to participate in his expeditions. He felt that everyone would remain more content if an intact family unit was maintained until the men went off on the sledging advances. Peary rewarded those who helped him with blankets, tools, weapons, and food.

Often hunters had to track game for many days before they found any in this desolate region. The end of a musk oxen shoot is shown above. Below is a map of some of Peary and Henson's Arctic routes.

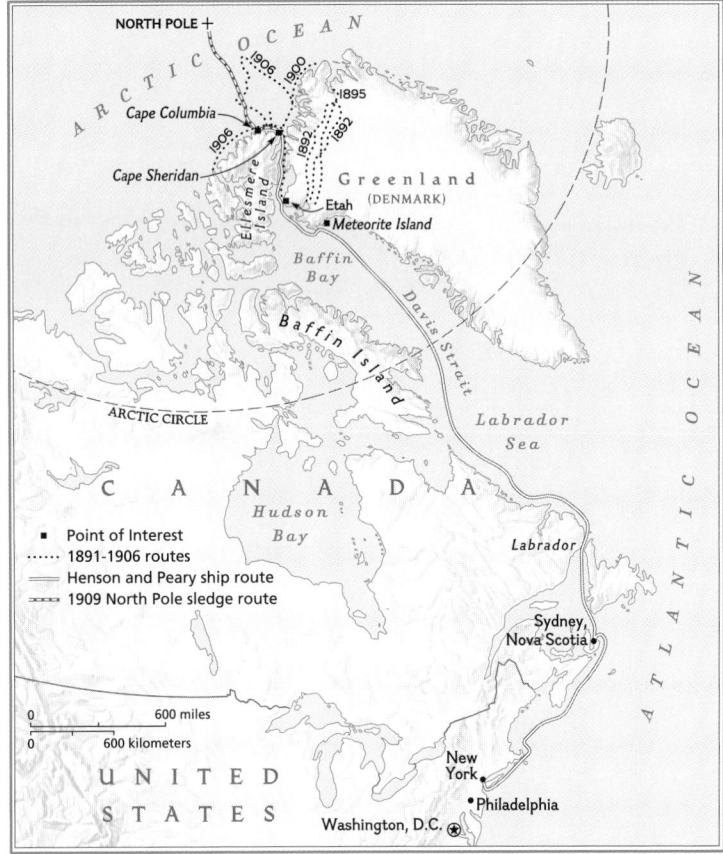

After the two men had killed several bulls, a wounded cow charged Peary. Peary fumbled to reload his shotgun as the cow came so close he could feel the heat of its breath. But in the last instant, Henson was able to down the animal with his own shot. The two men butchered the game and sledged the meat back to camp and a nearly starved Lee.

Even then, the men were not out of danger. Storms again delayed them, and their new supply of food did not last. Only one of the dogs remained. Lee could no longer walk, so Peary and Henson had to place harnesses around themselves to pull him on a sledge. For 125 miles they dodged pressure ridges—heaps of broken ice—and crevasses they could barely detect in the fog. The men finally staggered back to base camp, all of them exhausted and nearly starving. Henson revived himself enough to reach the closest Inuit settlement. From there he sent some men back to Lee and Peary with food and healing herbs. All three men were eventually nursed back to health.

Peary was devastated by the thought of another failure. He heard, while in the Inuit settlement, that the Swedish explorer

Fridtjof Nansen had penetrated within 230 miles of the Pole, the farthest north thus far. He had serious competition to contend with.

When the *Kite* came to retrieve the men, Peary insisted that the ship sail down the Greenland coast to pick up three meteorites, masses of stone and metal that had fallen from outer space. For years, the Inuit had worshiped these "iron mountains" and used the metal in them to make weapons and tools. They were so protective of the meteorites that they kept the location secret. Peary felt that bringing the stones to America would be so important scientifically that it would help him get another leave of absence from the Navy and raise funds for another expedition. He bribed two Inuit men to reveal the location.

After three days of struggle, the two meteorites called the "Dog" and the "Woman," weighing a half-ton and three tons, respectively, were placed in the *Kite's* hold. Henson and Peary made two more trips to Greenland in 1896 and 1897 to get the third meteorite, called the "Tent." Estimated at thirty-five tons, it was the largest meteorite known in the world.

When they got home, Josephine Peary sold the meteorites to the American Museum of Natural History in New York for $40,000. Henson found work at the same museum, preparing displays of animals in Arctic settings.

Henson was beginning to become aware of his newly acquired responsibilities. Previously, he had thought that arriving first at the Pole would be a great personal accomplishment. It would be an adventure like none other and would make him part of history. But after talking to friends who were more political, he began to realize how important it would be for all African Americans if a black man was one of the first to set foot at the North Pole. He became even more determined.

However, Henson's personal life was crumbling. Eva Henson had grown weary of her husband's long absences. When Henson and Peary finally returned to the States with the last meteorite, they had been away for a total of four years. Eva asked for a divorce. Henson agreed, and their marriage ended in 1897.

Peary began to seek funding for his next trip. He reasoned that he would be more successful if he could build a ship strong enough to force its way through the dense, ice-strewn water of Baffin Bay. The closer he could get to the Pole by ship, the more likely his success. A British newspaper publisher presented him with a ship—the *Windward*—but a machinist's strike prevented

"As usual I was a member of the party, and my back still aches when I think of the hard work I did to help load that monster aboard the *Hope*."

The "Dog" meteorite, weighing a half ton, and the "Woman," weighing three tons, were removed from Meteorite Island in Greenland by rolling them and dragging them to shore with ropes—see the photo at left above. An attempt was made to remove the thirty-five-ton meteorite called the "Tent" in 1896 with hydraulic jacks. But Peary and Henson failed. The men had to use steel rails to propel it across a stretch of water toward the *Hope* in 1897, as seen in the photo at top right and below.

the installation of the necessary powerful engines. Peary set sail anyway.

In July 1898, just three men—Peary, Henson, and a doctor named T. S. Dedrick, Jr.—sailed for Ellesmere Island in the Canadian Arctic, which Peary determined was a better base than Greenland. Stormy weather in Princess Marie Bay forced the group, accompanied with a small Inuit crew, to be trapped in the ice miles from their intended base camp. But in January 1899, the men were able to sledge supplies to Fort Conger on Ellesmere, an existing base camp located as far north as they could penetrate. Peary's feet became frostbitten during several days of advances in extreme conditions. Eight of his toes snapped off at the first joint when his boots were removed at the fort. The men stayed at Fort Conger until Peary's severe pain had diminished enough so that he could be moved.

Six weeks later, Henson lashed Peary to a sledge for the grueling 11-day trip back to the ship. On board, Dr. Dedrick had to amputate all but the little toes on both feet. After weeks of recuperation, Peary and Henson returned to Fort Conger, transferring the last of the supplies from the ship.

When the *Windward* sailed for the United States in August 1899, no one from the expedition was on board. Peary, Henson, and Dr. Dedrick all remained in Etah, Greenland, where the doctor deserted the expedition to live in an Inuit settlement. The ship was not scheduled to return to retrieve Henson and Peary until 1901. While in the Arctic, the explorers made several more attempts at the Pole, both from Fort Conger on Ellesmere Island and from a northern point of Greenland, but they only got as far as what they called the "Big Lead."

The "Big Lead" was where the land ice ended and the polar sea ice began. Depending upon the degree of its salt content, seawater freezes at approximately 28.6°F, or a temperature lower than that at which pure water freezes. When the ice begins to melt, it melts due to the radiation transmitted by the rays of the sun rather than the air temperature. As the summer nears, the pack ice at the edge of the land begins to melt, exposing a river of dark freezing water swirling

Above: *Windward*, which proved to be underpowered for Arctic navigation, is trapped in ice.

Advertisements attempted to entice riders to the railroads. The ads suggested that the traveler could be pampered by the services of the Pullman porter, typically an uneducated black man.

below. Nothing was more exasperating for the explorers than having to wait for temperatures to fall low enough so that a bridge of ice formed over the lead. Their only other choice was to try to navigate around, which might take them miles off course. This time, they chose to go back to base.

When the two returned to the United States in 1902, they found that the public had grown weary of their failures, making raising money for another attempt harder than ever. But Peary did not give up. He worked tirelessly raising funds to build a new, reinforced ship, one that would be even stronger than the *Windward*. He hoped this vessel would be able to smash its way through the ice and bring the expedition closer to its goal.

Meanwhile, Henson needed work. He signed on to be a Pullman porter on the Pennsylvania Railroad. A porter handled baggage and served passengers on railroad sleeping cars. Henson figured that train travel would show him a world he had not yet seen. He was dismayed to find that the frozen, bleak Arctic was more hospitable than his own country. Men insulted him with racial slurs and threw objects at him when the train traveled in the South. One night, in Florida, a man with a shotgun blew out the train window above his head.

American society was changing as people left the farms for industrial work in the cities. Women could not yet vote, airplanes had not yet flown, but automobiles were slowly taking the place of horses. And in 1896, the U.S. Supreme Court ruled that it was legal for local governments to segregate, or separate, African Americans from white people. Some governments restricted races from mixing in schools, hospitals, means of transportation, restaurants, recreation, marriage, and other institutions.

When Peary finally got his reinforced ship, named the *Roosevelt*, he summoned Henson to New York to help prepare for the next voyage. By this time,

The specially built ship, the *Roosevelt*, contributed to the expedition's eventual success because it got the crew members closer to the North Pole than any previous ship. Here the ship is being unloaded of its cargo, after proceeding so far north it became trapped in the ice.

Henson was almost 40, and he had begun to question the direction his life had taken. He had no family or place to call home. Newspaper accounts deemed his work with Peary worthless. He was continually forced to take menial jobs and had very little money. He was feeling like a fish out of water in the United States. He felt so much more at home in the chilly Arctic, among people whom he loved, in a challenge for which he felt destined. Yet even this choice was not within his control. He could only explore the Arctic when Lieutenant Peary sponsored him.

Then Henson met a young bank clerk named Lucy Jane Ross and began to court her. By the time the *Roosevelt* was ready to sail out of New York, in July

33

Inuit women carried their children in packs on their backs. Above is Akatingwah, wife of Ooblooyah. Below is a representation of a crewman's day's rations in pemmican, fuel, and biscuits.

1905, Henson had forgotten how unsatisfied he had been with his personal and professional lives. He asked Lucy to marry him. She said she would when he returned from his next trip.

Henson was confident this sixth mission to the Pole would be successful. The *Roosevelt* was reinforced to hammer through the frozen sea. Her hull was egg-shaped, designed to squeeze above the ice. Her 1,000-horsepower steam engines could power through the cakes of ice that would dot their path. The hope was that this new ship would be able to deposit the expedition on the rim of the frozen sea, close to the Pole.

The *Roosevelt*, captained by Robert Bartlett, took three weeks to fight its way from Etah, Greenland, to Cape Sheridan on Ellesmere Island, arriving on September 5, 1905. The sea ice lifted the ship and rattled her like a creaking, squealing toy. Sheets of ice under her keel raised the ship and dropped her onto thinner ice with a shudder, all the way to Cape Sheridan. Yet the *Roosevelt* managed to advance 350 miles farther north than the *Windward* had ever gone. The North Pole was only 500 miles away.

Peary was constantly revising his techniques to succeed in his assault on the Pole. In past attempts, he had avoided winter's frigid temperatures, which could plummet to between 50 and 70 degrees below zero, and had begun his treks in the summer. However, when the snow melts into slush and mud, sledging becomes more dangerous.

Matthew Henson poses carrying a pack and snowshoes on his back.

"It is well known that the chief characteristic of Commander Peary is persistency which, coupled with fortitude, is the secret of his success."

During the 1905–1906 expedition, a group of seven men pose for a photo to commemorate their achievement of setting the farthest north record to that time. Peary carried flags with him at all times to display at memorable occasions such as this.

A fall into icy water rather than onto banks of snow can create a deadly chill for both man and dogs. Peary planned this new expedition to begin in midwinter and end before the spring thaw.

Before they left the United States, Peary had had pemmican—a food made of ground meat and animal fat—manufactured as the main food for the men and dogs. The human version was enriched with currants and spices to enhance its taste and was eaten cold like salami. The explorers also carried tea, cracker-like biscuits, and condensed milk.

On March 1, 1906, Peary sent Henson out to break the trail. Henson was elated because he felt that Peary finally appreciated his skills. Peary later said of Henson, "He is a better dog driver and can handle a sledge better than any man living, except some of the best Eskimo hunters. I couldn't get along without him…." But leads and storms on the trail stopped the expedition.

The men made camp in igloos they built by the sides of the leads while the ice constantly creaked and groaned beneath them. They slept fitfully with the threat that the sledges, equipment, and the men themselves could be tossed into the freezing water below as new leads opened around them. And days wasted by an open lead meant that the teams were running out of fuel, food, and possibilities.

Six days later, ice floes finally formed, and the men and dogs dashed

Much of the warm spirit and decent character that endeared him to many of the people he encountered, such as the Inuit and the people who became his benefactors, is shown in this candid photo of Matthew Henson. It was shot on the deck of the *Roosevelt*.

across the leads. Despite the threat of starvation, Peary decided to make a mad dash to beat the record for farthest north. They abandoned all unnecessary equipment and sent nonessential teams back to the ship. They crawled through canyons of ice and over a treacherous series of pressure ridges. On the fifty-second day of the expedition, April 21, Peary took a reading by sextant of the sun's position and realized that they had set a new record for farthest north at 87°6'—about 174 nautical miles from the Pole. (Peary did all of his navigation using nautical miles, so those are the figures quoted in this book. One nautical mile is 1.15 statute, or standard, miles).

Matthew Henson plays with a young musk ox. Henson took pride in his rapport with the Arctic animals. He felt that sledge dogs were an indispensable part of survival in the Arctic, and early on he became a skilled sledge driver.

Even the retreat was dangerous. The Big Lead, which had delayed the expedition in 1902, caught them again. When Henson and Peary finally reached the *Roosevelt*, they looked like gaunt skeletons. They had spent 80 days in what amounted to another failure.

Over the course of many expeditions to the North Pole, both Henson and Peary had spent years living among the Inuit. During the summer of 1906, an Inuit woman named Aleqasina gave birth on board the *Roosevelt* to a son. The boy, named Kali, was fathered by Robert Peary and was Aleqasina's and Peary's second son. Anaukaq, their first child, had been born six years earlier. Within days, a son Henson fathered, also named Anaukaq, was born to an Inuit woman named Akatingwah. Despite the births, the two explorers left their new families behind when they sailed to America. In Henson's case, Akatingwah had been promised in marriage to an Inuit man. And Lucy Jane Ross would be waiting for him on the dock when they arrived back in the States. Both men promised to return, if only to try again for the North Pole.

Henson had hoped to marry Lucy Ross as soon as he returned, but he had "it'll work if God, wind, leads, ice, snow, and all the hells of this damned frozen land are willing."

to wait for nine months while he lived on the *Roosevelt* in New York harbor as the ship was being repaired for the next expedition. When the *Roosevelt* was finally moved out of dry dock in September 1907, Henson and Lucy were married.

Henson had great confidence in his new marriage, but he wasn't as keen on his new expedition. Together he and Peary had spent 16 years in and out of the Arctic region, only to meet with failure every time. He was receiving only $25 (about $500 today) a month in salary while preparing the *Roosevelt* to sail. Peary had been having difficulty raising funds. The public was calling him a madman and declaring that money given him was as good as poured down the drain. Yet Peary had the backing of President Theodore Roosevelt, who considered the naval officer a patriot and a hero. Roosevelt promoted him to Commander. By May 1908, the Commander had acquired enough money to plan a departure.

Other than Henson and Peary, Ross Marvin, a young engineer, and Robert Bartlett, the captain of the *Roosevelt*, were the only crew members who returned for this new expedition. Newcomers were George Borup, an athlete; Dr. John D. Goodsell, a surgeon; and Donald MacMillan, a teacher. The newcomers seemed to view the coming adventure as a sporting event. Henson, who by this time was 42 years old, thought differently. He had devoted practically his whole adult life to the mission. He had teetered close to death. He had lost, and nearly lost, fellow crew members who had fallen into crevasses or the inky black waters of an Arctic Ocean lead. And he had sacrificed a stable family life so that he could be part of history. This was serious business. Yet Henson's mood brightened by the time the ship arrived at Etah, Greenland. He was to be reunited with his Inuit friends once again.

After Henson and Peary persuaded Inuit families to join the expedition, they all sailed to Cape Sheridan in an ice-busting, gut-wrenching voyage that took two weeks. Then the men unloaded the ship and sledged the supplies to Cape Columbia, on Ellesmere, which was only 413 miles south of the Pole.

By February 1909, the entire expedition was prepared to begin the march to the Pole. The novices had practiced their sledging and hunting and had spent enough time outdoors to prime themselves for the frigid Arctic conditions.

Left: The expedition's specially built ship, the *Roosevelt*, was trapped in the Arctic ice for months. When a vessel is hemmed in by the ice, there are dangers, because the ice pack is constantly shifting and grinding. A ship may be crushed in its grasp.

Henson supervised the Inuit women in the preparation and sewing of the garments the crew would wear. Each man had a long red flannel shirt and soft bearskin trousers lined with flannel. The soft cloth absorbed sweat and kept the roughness of the fur away from the skin. The pants were wrapped with a band of bearskin that held the legs snugly. A deerskin coat with a hood covered the torso. Bearskin mittens and sealskin boots completed the wardrobe. The outfit was easily transformed into a fur-lined sleeping sack.

On past expeditions, Commander Peary had sent sledges forward to store provisions along the trail. But he realized how unreliable that technique could be if the supplies got buried in deep snow. On this expedition, Peary proposed that a pioneering team would break the trail up ahead. Then six relay teams would follow, each carrying enough food, tools, weapons, and clothes for the whole expedition for five days. The entire expedition would consume supplies from the equivalent of one of the sledges. When those provisions were gone, one team and the weakest dogs would be sent back to headquarters. Until the actual participants of the last relay team were sent back, no one but Commander Peary would know who was to accompany him to the Pole.

Bartlett and Borup were sent out to break the trail. Then Henson and his Inuit team were sent out. Marvin, Goodsell, MacMillan and their teams followed, with Peary trailing. The Commander stayed in touch with the units by leaving notes in igloos for retreating teams so that they could forward information to teams bringing up more supplies.

The assault began with difficulty. Between March 2nd and 3rd, the temperature fell so low that no one got much sleep. The men had to beat their arms and feet to keep the blood circulating. The next day, the only way the crews could advance was to use their pickaxes to carve through rough ice studded with pressure ridges and sharp hummocks, or projections of ice. Some sledges broke

Above: Matthew Henson stands in front of an igloo built of slabs of ice placed in a spiral pattern to create a cone shape. A small opening (lower right) was left for entry. The temperature inside could rise as high as 50 degrees warmer than outside if a lamp was lit and body heat warmed the air.

The sledge teams had to confront pressure ridges and steep hummocks of ice, tremendous obstacles in their effort to reach the North Pole. Often they had to lift the sledges and dogs to go forward. Stormy weather, blinding snow, and wide expansive leads would often stop onward progress completely.

down, and the drivers often had to prod the dogs forward when they balked. Harsh winds stung their faces. Giant fissures in the ice threatened every step.

Henson's party followed Bartlett's tracks as far as the Big Lead. While camped beside the lead, the men awoke to the thunderous crack of shifting ice grinding beneath them. The Inuit considered this the evil work of Torngak, the devil. At any moment, men, equipment, and dogs could be thrown into the flowing water that was passing below. The crews shifted their campsite.

The team waited six days for the icy path spreading across the lead to freeze solid. They then advanced four days' marches until they caught up with Bartlett, who was stopped again by another wide lead. They had to set up camp and wait.

On March 11, a passable lane across the lead finally formed. But steep, rocky ice ridges studded the trail, and their supply of fuel was dwindling. One by one, the supporting parties and their Inuit crews were sent back to base camp to conserve the remaining fuel and supplies.

"No other but a Peary party would have attempted to travel in such weather. Our breath was frozen to our hoods of fur and our cheeks and noses frozen... it was a night of Plutonian Purgatory."

Robert Peary, an engineer, used his training to reconfigure the design of the Inuit sledge so that it could carry heavier loads and be more durable. Henson was instrumental in building the sledges that Peary designed, and repairing those that disintegrated in the below zero temperatures.

First, Dr. Goodsell was sent back with his team, and then MacMillan. Borup was sent back on March 20. The remaining crew crossed plains of deep ice littered with pressure ridges and ice rubble. The temperature rose to 20 degrees below zero that turned the ice hard and smooth. But the warmer temperature opened up more leads.

Marvin finished five marches, and then Bartlett moved up again as the trail breaker. The temperature dropped. On March 26, a disappointed Marvin was ordered back to land. The expedition had gotten past Peary's record of farthest north. Then on March 30 Bartlett was told to retreat. Bartlett was so frustrated by not being picked to go all the way to the Pole that he walked 5 or 6 miles farther north to reach the 88th parallel, the record up until that date. It was only at Bartlett's departure that Henson knew he would accompany Peary to the North Pole.

The final assault team was made up of Henson, Peary, and the Inuit Ootah, Ooqueah, Egingwah, and Seegloo. Henson, Ootah, and Ooqueah were to break the trail over the last 133 miles. Peary, still crippled by the frostbite that had taken his toes 11 years earlier, took turns riding Egingwah's sledge and walking beside it. The conditions varied from stretches of smooth ice to steep ice ridges. Henson lengthened his marches to a back-breaking 18 to 20 hours a day. Peary caught up to Henson's team at day's end on April 1.

On April 5, Peary checked the position of the sun with his sextant. It told him that the Pole was only 35 miles away. The next morning, he alerted Henson to begin the march. Henson's progress was so successful that by

Top: Peary's journals recording the day he and Henson and the four Inuit finally reached their goal. The entry at left says, "The Pole at last!!! The prize of three centuries. My dream and goal for 20 years. Mine at last!" Right: Josephine Peary sewed by hand American flags that Robert Peary wore under his shirt during every expedition. This photo shows the handmade flag Peary asked Henson to place atop a pressure ridge to commemorate reaching the North Pole.

"It was as glorious and as inspiring a banner as any battle-scarred, blood-stained standard of the world …"

Peary had Matthew Henson and the four Inuit, Seegloo, Egingwah, Ooqueah, and Ootah, pose for photographs holding the four banners he carried to commemorate their reaching the North Pole. The Inuit were amazed that the culmination of so many years of effort was just another expanse of ice. "There is nothing here," Ootah said.

the time he had covered 20 miles, he was an hour ahead of Peary. As Henson drove his team across thin ice bridging a lead, the ice suddenly cracked. Henson, along with his dogs and sledge, was plunged into the frigid water. Henson began floundering about, trying to grasp onto jutting ice to save himself. He swallowed frigid water, and his lungs felt like they would burst. Then he found himself being lifted out of the water. It was Ootah who saved him and his sledge and dogs. Ootah slipped off Henson's wet boots and warmed his feet in the Inuit way, against Ootah's bare stomach.

They continued the march for four more hours until Henson deduced that they must have reached the North Pole. Henson, who had learned to steer a ship by the stars, had often played a game with Peary that he could estimate their position at the end of marches. "Knowing that we had kept on going in practically a straight line, [I] was sure that we had more than covered the necessary distance to insure our arrival at the top of the earth," wrote Henson later. He, Ooqueah and Ootah built igloos.

Peary arrived forty-five minutes later. When the clouds parted in the sky, he was able to take a latitude sighting with his sextant that affirmed they were at 89°57'. (The North Pole is at 90° N.) They probably got as close to determining their position as their navigational gear allowed—within five miles of the North Pole. For all intents and purposes, the expedition had reached its goal. It was April 6, 1909. In a whisper, Peary announced his reading to Henson. Then the two explorers, weary with the culmination of so many years of effort, crawled into an igloo, lay down, and went to sleep.

When Peary awoke, he wrote in his diary, "The Pole at last!!!" He unpacked a thin silk American flag he had been carrying with him all of his many years of exploration and planted it on top of his igloo.

Peary, Egingwah, and Seegloo then sledged several miles beyond the camp, covering a rectangular area, to ensure that an inaccurate reading would not spoil their achievement. Peary had Henson thrust an American flag into a large pressure ridge, and he took a photo of the five men holding flags that the Commander had carried with him for the occasion. Henson held an American flag that Josephine Peary had sewn by hand. Ooqueah held a flag of the Navy League. Ootah held a banner from Peary's college fraternity. Seegloo waved a flag of the Red Cross. And Egingwah held a Daughters of the American Revolution peace flag. They all joined in an exhilarated chorus of "Hip, hip, hooray." Then Peary said, "Let us go home, Matt."

Henson alone led the way south in a rapid race. The spring warming was threatening their path with menacing channels of open water. In his single first return march, Henson covered the distance of three northward marches. Their fast progress was possible because no broad leads deterred them, the trail was already broken, igloos were in position, and the sledges carried much lighter loads. Sixteen days after leaving the Pole, all six men managed to drag themselves into an empty igloo camp at Cape Columbia. When the men finally sledged back to the *Roosevelt*, they heard the distressing news that Ross Marvin had fallen into a lead on his retreat and died.

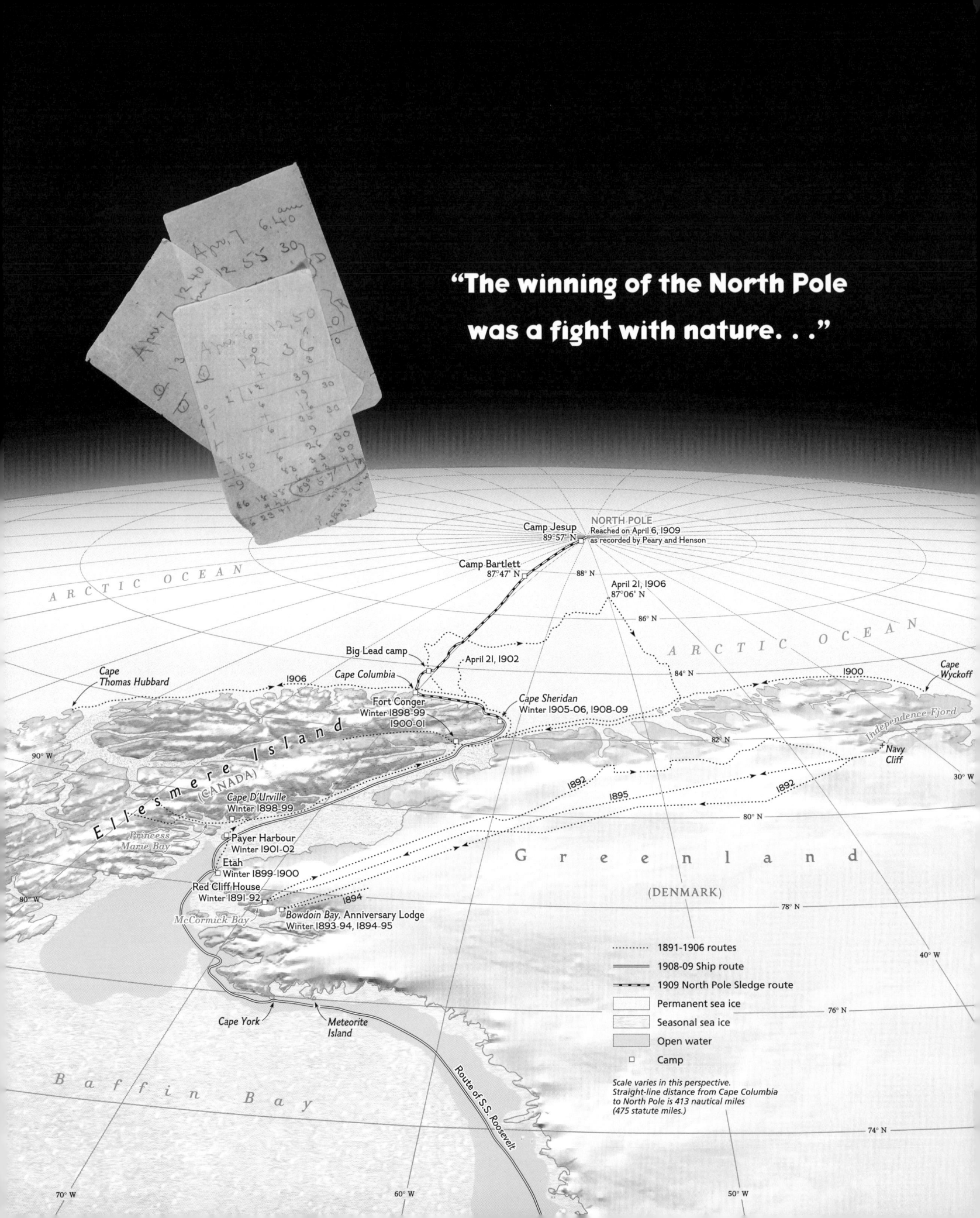

"The winning of the North Pole was a fight with nature..."

NORTH POLE
Reached on April 6, 1909
as recorded by Peary and Henson

Camp Jesup 89°57' N
Camp Bartlett 87°47' N
April 21, 1906 — 87°06' N
Big Lead camp
April 21, 1902
Cape Columbia
Cape Thomas Hubbard
1906
Fort Conger — Winter 1898-99, 1900-01
Cape Sheridan — Winter 1905-06, 1908-09
Cape Wyckoff
1900
Independence Fjord
Navy Cliff
1892
1895

Ellesmere Island (CANADA)

Cape D'Urville — Winter 1898-99
Princess Marie Bay
Payer Harbour — Winter 1901-02
Etah — Winter 1899-1900
Red Cliff House — Winter 1891-92
McCormick Bay
Bowdoin Bay, Anniversary Lodge — Winter 1893-94, 1894-95
1894

Greenland (DENMARK)

Cape York
Meteorite Island
Route of S.S. Roosevelt

Baffin Bay

Legend:
- ········ 1891-1906 routes
- ——— 1908-09 Ship route
- ━━━ 1909 North Pole Sledge route
- Permanent sea ice
- Seasonal sea ice
- Open water
- □ Camp

Scale varies in this perspective.
Straight-line distance from Cape Columbia to North Pole is 413 nautical miles (475 statute miles.)

It took several months for the ice to melt enough that the *Roosevelt* could break free and return to Etah. When they finally arrived on August 17, 1909, they received some more unsettling news. Dr. Frederick Cook, the same Dr. Cook who had set Peary's broken leg on his very first expedition, had sent a telegram from the Shetland Islands stating: "Reached North Pole April 21, 1908. Discovered land far north." In Etah, Henson had a chance to question the two Inuit who had accompanied Cook. They said they had made a short march onto the polar sea, built igloos, taken pictures, and only *claimed* to reach the Pole.

Henson, confident the achievement of his quest would not be questioned, prepared to say goodbye to his Inuit friends. He divided his personal belongings among those who had served him. Then he told them that, regretfully, he would never return. His Inuit son, Anaukaq, later proclaimed that Henson was the most popular man ever to visit the land.

On August 26, the *Roosevelt* headed south. From Labrador, Peary sent a telegram to the *New York Times* that simply read: "Stars and Stripes nailed to the Pole." Henson sent one to his wife that promised he was coming home for good.

Peary left the ship at North Sydney, Cape Breton, Canada, to continue

Left: Robert Peary kept notebooks that recorded his expeditions' advances to the Pole. He used a sextant to estimate his position by celestial bodies. A lead weight attached to piano wire enabled him to make soundings of the ocean's depth. The map details the actual achievements. Top: Matthew Henson sitting on one of his sledges after reaching the Pole

On September 16, 1909, a swarm of newspaper reporters surrounded Matthew Henson upon his final return to America aboard the *Roosevelt*. The reporters questioned Henson on details of Peary's versus Cook's claims on reaching the North Pole first. The newspaper background explores the controversy.

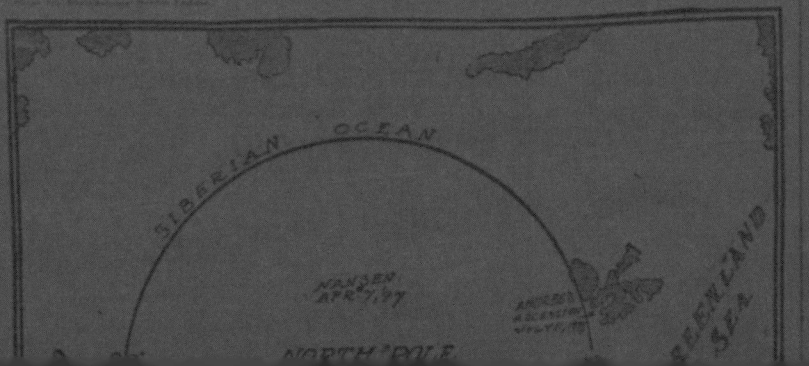

home by rail. Henson stayed on the ship to New York, where he was met by a horde of newspaper reporters eagerly seeking confirmation of Dr. Cook's claim, which Henson vigorously denied. Peary denied Cook's claim as well, wiring the *New York Times* the message, "Cook has handed the world a gold brick." But the public tended to believe the more cordial Dr. Cook over the gruff Peary, even though the doctor did not immediately return to America to provide details or proof of his trip.

Dr. Frederick Cook received a warm public reception when he returned to the United States after claiming by telegram: "Reached North Pole April 21, 1908." This was a year before Peary claimed he had achieved the goal.

Peary was devastated that the achievement of his lifelong goal had been so horribly spoiled. The Commander went to Maine, speaking to no one. There he busied himself preparing evidence proving that he had arrived at the North Pole first. When charming Dr. Cook finally returned to America, he was celebrated at banquets, given thousands of dollars to publish his story, and paid handsomely to speak about his triumph. This was despite the fact that Cook offered no proof of his expedition's success.

When Henson arrived in New York early in October 1909, he found that his wife had quit her job in expectation of the rewards her husband would receive for arriving first at the North Pole. But the public didn't believe Henson and Peary. They discounted the testimonies of MacMillan, Captain Bartlett, and the other white members of the expedition. Henson went on a speaking tour to explain the Peary side of the controversy. However, his audiences tended to be unsympathetic and hostile, occasionally booing him off the stage. He was jeered as the ignorant black man Peary took north for a witness so that he could conceal the fact that he hadn't reached the Pole.

Embarrassed, Henson quit the tour. When he returned to New York, he had to find a job. No longer could he contact Commander Peary and ask for work. Communication between the two had ceased. No one is sure why.

Supporters of Cook suggested Peary dismissed Henson to suppress the lie they shared. Supporters of Henson suspected that it was because Henson might have gotten to the Pole first, and Peary didn't want to acknowledge that fact. Once their business relationship was over, perhaps Peary did not feel compelled to maintain any other relationship.

That fall, a three-member subcommittee from the National Geographic Society held a meeting to investigate evidence submitted by Peary. In November 1909, the subcommittee issued a statement in which they unanimously agreed that Commander Robert E. Peary had reached the North Pole first. The National Geographic awarded him their highest honor, a special gold Hubbard Medal. Finally, in January 1910, the University of Copenhagen declared Cook a fraud. Peary was promoted to Rear Admiral in the Navy and retired on a pension of almost $8,000 a year ($156,000 today). Soon the world's geographic societies were giving him honors and medals. Congress passed a resolution that officially thanked Admiral Peary for his Arctic explorations. Yet not one of the honors or medals even mentioned Matthew Henson's name.

Dr. Frederick Cook's claim of reaching the North Pole first was finally discounted in January 1910. Here Peary is being accorded honors during a visit to London during that same year.

Matt Henson, Who Reached Pole With Peary in 1909, Dies at 88

He Was the Only With Explorer Dash to 190

Matthew (Matt) Henson, the man A E. Peary termed in his final five-day North Pole, died h at St. Clare's Hospital. The 88 year-old explorer American to acco ral Peary to th cumbed of a cer rhage.

First reports i Admiral Peary had panied only by Es When the party r for Mr. Henson's also was recorded

Mr. Henson, who had been hired by Admiral valet, accompanied the explorer on all of his expeditions over a twenty-two-year period. In interviews after the completion of the mission on April 7, 1909, Admiral Peary said:

"This position I have given

enson in 1950, e was honored at Pentagon for exploits.

Top: Henson is shown in 1926, at age 59. Below: President Dwight D. Eisenhower honors Henson and his wife, Lucy, in 1954 at a reception. Henson's obituary is in the background.

Matthew Henson's courage, tenacity, and good nature allowed him to be the perfect partner to Robert Peary in their achievement of being the first explorers to reach the North Pole.

Booker T. Washington, of Alabama's Tuskegee Institute, and Adam Clayton Powell, Sr., an influential minister, represented the African-American community by celebrating Henson at a banquet. There they gave him a gold watch and called him a hero for his entire race. Yet the general public considered Henson to be only the "Negro manservant" who went with Admiral Peary to the North Pole.

With effort, Henson found a job parking cars in Brooklyn. Then some black politicians and some of Henson's friends persuaded President Taft to award Henson the job of messenger boy at the U.S. Customs House in New York City. While he worked there, Henson wrote his autobiography, *A Negro Explorer at the North Pole*. Robert Peary agreed to write the preface and introduced Henson to his own publisher, Frederick A. Stokes Company, who published the book in 1912.

On February 20, 1920, Admiral Robert Edwin Peary died. It is said that when told of the death, Henson went off by himself and cried. In 1937, when he was 70, Henson retired from his messenger job with a pension of $1,020 a year. Slowly, organizations and civic bodies began to honor him. In 1944, Congress issued a medal honoring members of the Peary expedition, including Henson. The next year, all the members of the expedition received the Navy Medal. President Eisenhower had a reception for Matthew Henson and his wife, Lucy, in the White House in 1954.

Matthew Alexander Henson died of a cerebral hemorrhage at age 88 on March 9, 1955. Thousands attended the memorial service. Lucy Henson had Henson buried in Woodlawn Cemetery in the Bronx, New York. Years later, Dr. S. Allen Counter, an African-American professor from Harvard, led the movement to honor Matthew Henson as the "Co-Discoverer of the North Pole." On April 6, 1988, 79 years after the conquest of the North Pole, Matthew Henson was reburied with full honors beside the monument and grave of Robert E. Peary, in Arlington National Cemetery. Lucy is buried alongside.

On Matthew Henson's tombstone the following is inscribed: "The lure of the Arctic is tugging at my heart. To me the trail is calling. The old trail. The trail that is always new."

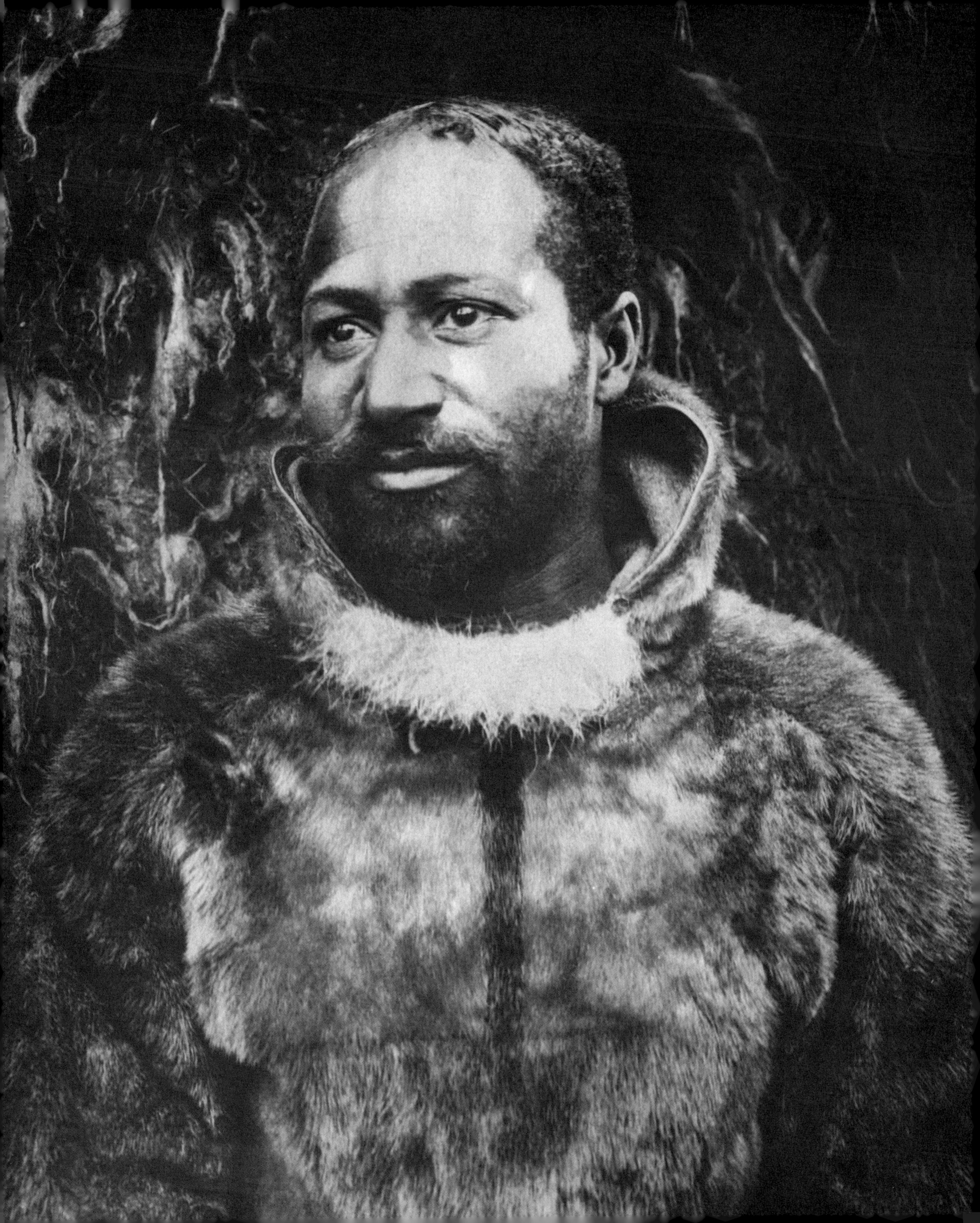

Anaukaq Henson is the son of Matthew Henson and an Inuit woman named Akatingwah. Anaukaq was 81 years old when he first visited the United States in 1987. He and other Inuit family members visited Henson's grave site in the Bronx, New York. He also met with some of his American relatives.

Afterword

In 1879 13-year old Matthew Alexander Henson made his first voyage around the world on the *Katie Hines,* where his appetite for adventure was born.

In 1886, when Robert Edwin Peary was a young man, he made his first trip to the Arctic. It was during that trip that his longing for further exploration was developed. Five years later these two would-be adventurers crossed paths and forged a partnership to achieve a mutual goal that took 23 years to accomplish. Their goal was to be the first to stand at the geographic marker known as the North Pole.

In their first trip to the Arctic together, a remarkable incident shaped their eventual approach. Peary and Henson, on a hunt, found themselves caught up in a severe storm. Tormented by the driving winds and blinded by stinging snow, Henson and Peary were only able to throw up a wall of hard-packed snow for shelter. They slept in sleeping bags, huddling together with the dogs, doing all that they could to conserve body heat. They did not know how to build an igloo and barely survived that tremendous trial. They regretted their lack of preparation and faulty equipment and worked very hard in future expeditions to correct their mistakes. The two men became inventive, creative, and resourceful in planning how they could master that unforgiving environment. The learned to use the Inuit model for their food, shelter, and transportation. They made eight attempts before they accomplished their mutual goal. In 2000, the National Geographic Society posthumously awarded their highest award, the Hubbard Medal, to Matthew Henson for distinction in "exploration, discovery, and research." (Peary had received his medal years earlier, in 1909.)

It was mainly because of Matthew Henson's intelligence, benevolence, and warm personality that he was able to forge a bond between two distinct and different cultures, the native Inuit and the North American white culture. Henson loved the Inuit and they loved him. It was the combination of

Top: The National Geographic Society posthumously awarded the gold Hubbard Medal to Matthew Henson in November 2000. Below: Henson, at 81, reads to a child from the first issue of the comic book series, *Negro Heroes,* which featured his adventure.

the contributions from these two cultures, and his own African-American culture, which achieved one of the world's last unexplored discoveries.

Matthew Henson lived during a period in America that is perhaps repugnant to our present sense of justice. Segregation separated white and black people in the South. African Americans were considered inferior and were expected to be subservient even though it was decades after slavery's end. Henson was referred to as Peary's "manservant" long after he had outgrown that status (and is still described that way in some contemporary stories of their explorations). What could possibly be the duties of a manservant in the frigid Arctic? Instead of waiting hand and foot on Peary, Henson actually sledged Peary for eleven days straight so that he could save what was left of the Commander's feet. That implies loyalty, devotion, and caring—not servitude.

Henson and Peary survived in the Arctic because they were willing to work together toward their mutual goal. Often at the point of starvation, they were known to split the last crumbs of the few remaining morsels of food they could scavenge. Yet, during the era in which they lived, they would not have been able to share a meal together in many restaurants, due to segregation.

Obviously it is Robert Peary's greatest legacy that he was one of the first men to step foot at the North Pole. But he has another legacy, as well. He overlooked the color of Matthew Henson's skin when he selected a partner to help him achieve his goal. He used who he thought was the best man for the job, despite society's suggestions that Henson was inadequate.

Matthew Henson's ultimate legacy, perhaps, is that he proved that courage, ability, and loyalty are not determined by the color of one's skin, but by the determination of one's spirit.

Ajako Henson, shown here with his wife, Puto, is the grandson of Matthew Henson.

Now it is almost one hundred years since these two courageous men accomplished their remarkable achievement. Much has changed. Travelers, by way of hot-air balloons, snow skis, submarines, and planes, among other means, have mastered the difficult North Pole. Even Matthew Henson's Inuit descendants now live in permanent houses in towns and settlements, rather than on the ice as nomads in igloos. But their respect for him is still as strong as when he lived among them.

Another of Matthew Henson's legacies is his descendants: the children, grandchildren, and great-grandchildren of his son, Anaukaq. They still talk reverently about Maripahluk, or "Matthew the Kind One." They are proud because they are descended from one of the most popular men in the Arctic, a great hunter, a great explorer. Matthew Henson was a remarkable man.

CHRONOLOGY

1866
Matthew Alexander Henson is born in Nanjemoy, Maryland, August 8.

1867
The Henson family moves to Washington, D.C.

1873
Matthew's mother dies.

1879
Matthew's father dies. Matthew leaves home to work in a restaurant. Then he sets off for Baltimore to seek work.

1879–83
Matthew sails on the *Katie Hines*.

1887
He assists Robert Peary on a Nicaraguan expedition.

The exploits of Robert E. Peary and Matthew A. Henson have become so popular that an educational company produced a game that honors the two explorers.

1891–92
Henson's first expedition in the Arctic

1893–95
Second expedition to northern Greenland achieving 77°23' north latitude.

1896 & 1897
Henson and Peary return to the Arctic to retrieve the large "Tent" meteorite.

1898–1902
Henson spends four years in the Arctic with Peary, achieving 84°17' north latitude.

1902
Henson returns to the U.S. and works as a Pullman porter. He becomes engaged to Lucy Jane Ross.

1905–06
Accompanies Peary to within 174 miles of the Pole, 87°6' north latitude.

1907
Marries Lucy Jane Ross

1909
Reaches the North Pole on April 6

1920
Admiral Peary dies.

1937
Henson retires from his messenger job at the U.S. Customs House in New York City, at age 70.

1944
Henson receives an award from Congress, along with all the American men of the expedition.

1945
Receives the Navy Medal

1955
Matthew Henson dies of a cerebral hemorrhage on March 9.

1988
Matthew Henson is reinterred next to Robert Peary at Arlington National Cemetery.

2001
Henson is posthumously awarded the National Geographic Society's Hubbard Medal.

BIBLIOGRAPHY & RESOURCES

Publications

Berton, Pierre. *The Arctic Grail, The Quest for the North West Passage and the North Pole, 1818-1909.* New York: Penguin Books, 1988.

Bryan, C.D.B. *The National Geographic Society: 100 Years of Adventure and Discovery.* New York: Harry N. Abrams, Inc., 1987.

Clark, William R. *Explorers of the World.* Garden City, New York: The Natural History Press, 1944.

Counter, S. Allen. *North Pole Legacy: Black, White and Inuit.* Montpelier, Vermont: Invisible Cities Press, 2001.

*Gilman, Michael. *Matthew Henson, Explorer (Black Americans of Achievement).* New York: Chelsea House Publishers, 1988.

Henson, Matthew A. *A Negro Explorer at the North Pole.* New York: Frederick A. Stokes Company, 1912.

Herbert, Wally. *Across the Top of the World.* New York: G.P. Putnam's Sons, 1975.

Herbert, Wally. "Did He Reach the Pole?" NATIONAL GEOGRAPHIC magazine. September, 1988, pp. 387–413.

Horwood, Harold. *Bartlett the Great Canadian Explorer.* Garden City, New York: Doubleday & Company, 1977.

Lewis, John Edwin. *Race for the Pole.* New York: Henry Holt and Co., 1960.

Ley, Willy and the Editors of Life. *The Poles.* New York: Time Incorporated, 1962.

*Litwin, Laura Baskes. *Matthew Henson, Co-Discoverer of the North Pole.* (African American Biographies). Berkeley Heights, New Jersey: Enslow Publishers, Inc., 2001.

Miller, Floyd. *Ahdoolo! The Biography of Matthew A. Henson.* New York: E.P. Hutton & Co., Inc., 1963.

Mountfield, David. *A History of Polar Exploration.* New York: The Dial Press, 1974.

Peary, Robert E. "Dash to the Pole." *Great Adventures with National Geographic: Exploring Land, Sea, and Sky.* Washington, D.C.: National Geographic, 1963.

Rasky, Frank. *The North Pole or Bust.* Toronto: McGraw-Hill Ryersin, Ltd, 1977.

Robinson, Bradley. *Dark Companion.* New York: Robert M. McBride & Company, 1947.

Stefansson, Vilhjalmur. *Great Adventures and Explorations.* New York: The Dial Press, 1947.

Steger, Will with Paul Schurke. *North to the Pole.* New York: Times Books, 1987.

Weems, John Edwin. *Race for the Pole.* New York: Henry Holt & Co., 1960.

Weems, John Edwin. *Peary, the Explorer and the Man.* London: Eyre & Spottiswoode, 1967.

Wright, Theon. *The Big Nail, the Story of the Cook-Peary Feud.* New York: The Johns Day, Company, 1970.

*An asterisk indicates a book intended for young readers.

Web sites

http://news.nationalgeographic.com/news/2003/01/0110_030113_henson.html

http://www.unmuseum.org/henson.htm

http://www.people.fas.harvard.edu/~counter/

Places to visit

Matthew Henson Earth Conservation Center, Washington, D.C.

Arlington National Cemetery Arlington, Virginia

Quotations from *Onward* are taken from the following sources:

Page 5: "The lure of the Arctic…" MH Gravestone, *A Negro Explorer at the North Pole*, by Matthew A. Henson, p. 95; Page 9 (full quote): "Moreover, Henson was the best man I had with me for this kind of work, with the exception of the Eskimos ….", *The North Pole; Its Discovery in 1909*, Peary Arctic Club, Cooper Square Press, 2001 (or also Frederick A. Stokes Company, 1910), p. 272; Page 14: "I'll go North with you sir…" Miller, *Adhoolo!*, by Floyd Miller, p. 23; Page 16: "It was in June…" *A Negro Explorer at the North Pole*, by Matthew A. Henson, p. 16; Page 19: "…the Esquimo travels…" *A Negro Explorer*, p. 35; Page 22: "… the journey to the Pole…" *A Negro Explorer* p. 78; Page 26: "…for periods covering more…" *A Negro Explorer*, p. 17; Page 30: "As usual I was a member…" *A Negro Explorer*, p. 18; Page 36: "It is well known…" *A Negro Explorer*, p. 18; Page 38: "He is a better dog driver…" *Dark Companion*, by Bradley Robinson, p. 262; Page 40: "It'll work if God…" NATIONAL GEOGRAPHIC magazine, 9/99, p. 397; Page 44: "No other but a Peary party …" *A Negro Explorer*, p. 50; Page 47: "It was as glorious…" *A Negro Explorer*, p. 72; Page 48: "There is nothing here," *Dark Companion*, by Bradley Robinson, p. 227; Page 49: "Knowing that we had kept on…" *A Negro Explorer*, p. 71; Page 49: "The Pole at last!!!…" *Peary, the Explorer and the Man*, by John Edward Weems, p. 270; Page 49: "Let us go home, Matt." *Dark Companion*, by Bradley Robinson, p. 228; Page 50: "The winning of the North Pole…" *A Negro Explorer*, p. 77; Page 51: "Reached North Pole April 21, 1908." *Adhoolo!*, by Floyd Miller, p. 189; Page 51: "Stars and Stripes nailed…" *Adhoolo!*, by Floyd Miller, p. 188; Page 53: "(Cook) has simply handed the public a gold brick." *The Noose of Laurels*, by Wally Herbert, p. 285.

INDEX

Photographs are indicated by **boldface**. If photographs are included within a page span, the entire span is boldface.

Akatingwah (Inuit woman) **34**, 39, 58
Aleqasina (Inuit woman) 39
Anaukaq (Inuit man) 39, 51
Andrade, Leila Savoy **6**, 7
Annadore (Inuit child) **19**
Annowkah (Inuit man) **21**
Astrup, Eivind 14, 20, 23, 24

Bartlett, Robert 34, 41-43, 46, 53
Borup, George 41, 42, 46

Cook, Frederick A. 14, 15, 51, 53, **53**, 54
Counter, S. Allen 56

Dedrick, T. S., Jr. 31
Dog sledges **2-3**, 20, **21**, **22**, **43**, **44-45**

Egingwah (Inuit man) 46, **48**, 49
Eisenhower, Dwight D. **55**

Flags **6**, **23**, **36-37**, **47**, **48**, 49

Gibson, Langdon 14
Goodsell, John D. 41, 42, 46

Henson, Ajako **61**
Henson, Anaukaq 39, 51, **58**, 61
Henson, Eva 14, 29
Henson, Lucy 33-34, 39, 41, 53, **55**, 56
Henson, Matthew A. **5**, **55**, **57**, **60**
  1891-1892 North Pole expedition 14-23
  1893-1895 North Pole expedition 23-29
  1898-1902 North Pole expedition 29, 31-32
  1905-1906 North Pole expedition 9, 33-40
  1908-1909 North Pole expedition 41-53
  childhood 8, 10
  driving sledge **1**, **2-3**
  employment 8-**14**, 29, 32, 56
  family **6**, 7, 24, 39, **58**, 61, **61**
  and Inuit people 18, 20, 51, 59
  lecture tour 23
  marriages 14, 29, 33-34, 39, 41
  reaching North Pole **48**, 48-49
  recognitions 7, **55**, 56, 59, **62**
  relationship with Peary 9, 53-54, 56, 59, 60-61
Henson, Puto **61**

Ikwah (Inuit man) 18
Inuit 18, 23, 29, 39
  families 24, **26-27**, **34**
  and Henson 18, 20, 24, 51, 59
  on North Pole expeditions 25, 41-42, 43, 46, 48, 49, 51

Kali (Inuit boy) 39
Kudlooktoo (Inuit boy) 24

Lee, Hugh 24, 25, 28

MacMillan, Donald 41, 42, 46, 53
Mané (Inuit woman) 18, **19**
Marvin, Ross 41, 42, 46, 49
Meteorites 29, **30**

Nansen, Fridtjof 29
National Geographic Society 7
  Hubbard Medal 7, 54, 59, **60**
  investigation of North Pole claims 54
Nicaragua survey 11, **12**, 13
  map 13
North Pole expeditions
  1891-1892 **14-23**
  1893-1895 **23-29**
  1898-1902 29, **31**, 31-32
  1905-1906 9, **33-40**
  1908-1909 **41-53**
  claims 53-54
  clothing 42
  food **34**, 38
  route maps 28, 50
Nowyahrtlik (Inuit child) **19**

Ooqueah (Inuit man) 46, **48**, 49
Ootah (Inuit man) 46, **48**, **48**, 49

Peary, Josephine 29
  flags she sewed **47**, 49
  on North Pole expeditions 14, **16-17**, **19**, 23, 25
Peary, Marie Ahnighito 23, **25**
Peary, Robert E. **25**
  1891-1892 North Pole expedition **14-23**
  1893-1895 North Pole expedition **23-29**
  1898-1902 North Pole expedition 29, **31**, 31-32
  1905-1906 North Pole expedition 9, **33-40**
  1908-1909 North Pole expedition **41-53**
  children 23, **25**, 39
  death 56
  employing Henson 11, **12**, 13
  fundraising 23, **24**, 32, 41
  journals **46**, 50
  reaching North Pole 49
  recognitions 7, **54**, **62**
  relationship with Henson 9, 53-54, 56, 59, 60-61
Powell, Adam Clayton, Sr. 56

Roosevelt, Theodore 41

Seegloo (Inuit man) 46, **48**, 49
Segregation 32, 60
Sharecroppers 8, **10**

Verhoeff, John T. 14, 20, 23

Washington, Booker T. 56

One of the world's largest non-profit scientific and educational organizations, the National Geographic Society was founded in 1888 "for the increase and diffusion of geographic knowledge." Fulfilling this mission, the Society educates and inspires millions every day through its magazines, books, television programs, videos, maps and atlases, research grants, the National Geographic Bee, teacher workshops, and innovative classroom materials. The Society is supported through membership dues, charitable gifts, and income from the sale of its educational products. This support is vital to National Geographic's mission to increase global understanding and promote conservation of our planet through exploration, research, and education.

For more information, please call 1-800-NGS LINE (647-5463) or write to the following address:

NATIONAL GEOGRAPHIC SOCIETY
1145 17th Street N.W.
Washington, D.C. 20036-4688
U.S.A.

Visit the Society's Web site:
www.nationalgeographic.com